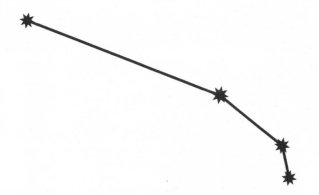

 ONE IDEA PRESS

Aries

a love letter

Heidi Rose Robbins

with illustrations by
Wyoh Lee

hello love.

(yes, you)

Friends,

I'm so glad you are holding this book! It is filled with encouragement and an ongoing invitation for us all to be more fully who we are.

The best way to work with these books is to purchase one for each of your signs — your Sun, Moon, and Rising Sign.

These are the three most important positions in your astrological chart. You can discover what these are if you enter your exact time, date, and place of birth in any online astrology site. Each position has something unique to offer.

When you read the book for your Moon, think of it as an energy that is very available to you. It's a place where you might feel comfortable. The Moon has to do with our emotional life, our patterns of behavior, and circumstances of our childhood. We can rely on the Moon, but we also want to work to shed the patterns that no longer serve us.

The Sun is our present personality. We can learn a lot about our everyday self in the world. We can learn about the energies we have readily available to us to use in service to our highest calling.

The Rising Sign is the most important point. It is the sign that was rising as we took our first breath. It holds the key to our soul's calling. It is an energy we want to cultivate and be generous with throughout our lives.

So — enjoy the journey. Be sure to read them all!

Welcome
{13}

11

My dear Aries,

This little book is a love letter to your feisty, fiery self. It is written to remind you of your many gifts. It is written to be a loving mirror so any page can remind you who you truly are. Take it in, dear Aries. Don't read too quickly. Don't skip ahead. I know how you like to keep things moving. But promise me you'll take the time to see your passionate and daring self in these pages.

This little book will also explore those places in ourselves that start to close when we want to open, the part of us that hesitates when we want to act. We all have our quirks and difficulties, after all. But if we return again and again to our potency, vulnerability, and sense of possibility, we can outgrow our closures one by one.

Think of this book as a treasure chest containing the golden coins of YOU. Open it when you wish to remember your beauty, worth or great potential. And remember, too, this Aries part of you is just one voice in the symphony of YOU. It cannot possibly contain your complexity and bounty. But it can begin to name just a few of your gifts.

Read this out loud when you can. Read this in the morning. Read it before bed. Read it when you need encouragement. Read it even if you are already feeling feisty. Let it fuel your fire. But READ IT. And own it! And use it! And claim it! This is your love letter, Aries. This is the song of YOU.

Big love,
Heidi Rose

Celebrating Aries

As you read this celebration, you will sometimes say "Yes, yes, yes! This is me!" And you may likewise sometimes feel that you have not yet lived into some of these qualities. This is honoring and celebrating the very best of your Aries energy. This is naming the full, conscious, awakened use of your Aries gifts. We are sounding the note of THE POSSIBLE. So, even if you feel you still have work to do in certain areas — as do we all — let these words be inspiration to offer your best Self!

You, my dear Aries, know
how to begin.

No one gets it going quite like
you. No one leads the way as you
do. You plunge, launch, activate,
inaugurate. You act on your ideas
without excessive deliberation.
You say, "The time is now," and
you leap.

You are bold, feisty
and daring.

You are not afraid to go forth,
to face what may obstruct
your path. You have vitality and
strength on your side and you are
willing to step into the unknown.
Others will call on you to make
the first move. You are brave,
dear Aries.

You are a true LEADER.

You are willing, able and love to lead. You sound the call and others follow. Your word and deed work together to launch. You are the first one to get the party started, get the work underway and say, "Now!" when others want to weigh all the options. You, dear Aries, are a rallying cry unto yourself.

You inspire progress.

You are a lover of the new and
the cutting edge. You have
ideas for our collective future.
You know we can do better. You
encourage everyone to cultivate
daring. You inspire action.
You inspire progress. You forge
a new path.

♈

You are a warrior.

Mars is one of your most important planets, Aries. And Mars is the warrior. YOU are a warrior. You will fight when called. You will fight for what's right. You do not hang back. You assert.

You have bold, innovative
ideas which you are meant
to share.

You are quick, sharp and
intelligent. You generate a ton
of great ideas. You spearhead
your own initiatives and offer
other ideas to friends, colleagues
and your community. You plant
seeds wherever you go and with
whomever you speak. You come
forth with the power of your mind.

Your vitality and springtime
self inspire others.

You have energy Aries. You have
gumption. You have lifeblood
flowing in your veins. You embody
Spring. You inspire others to wake
up and LIVE. You fan the flames
in others, always helping them
begin again.

You know how to bust
through any obstacle.

You break on through to the other
side. Very little will deter you.
Red Rover, Red Rover is every
Aries' favorite game. Like the
Ram, you crash and bash and
repeat until you've succeeded.
You are a forerunner.

♈

You are your own best boss.

You like to be in charge, Aries.
You are good at taking the reins.
You know what you need to do.
Go ahead and lead the way.
Don't wait for your marching
orders. Hire yourself as the CEO
of your own life.

You are dynamic.

You are charismatic and
energetic, dear Aries. You are
lively and engaged. You leave
VITALITY in your wake. You
activate the potential in others.
You embody fire and ignite that
fire in all you meet.

♈

You are forever young at heart.

Aries, you are the first sign of the zodiac. You are youth and springtime and new beginnings. No physical age gets you down. You carry the capacity to start over. Your young self is forever within you cheering you on.

You know that each day is new and each day we can be new unto ourselves.

Your super-charged rocket powers launch us into new chapters.

Never underestimate your power to get us all moving. Never underestimate your fire. You carry the spark that ignites the greater flame. Your break open the doors to all the new chapters in our lives.

♈

You know how to sprint.

Aries, you know how to run short distances with great enthusiasm and power. It's sometimes more difficult for you to complete the marathon. But you thrive and dive into potent, achievable, 'sprintable' goals.

♈

You say, "If not me, then who?"
and "If not now, then when?"

You seize the day. You say Yes.
You do not shirk the call. You are
willing to be imperfect as long as
you get underway. You recognize
there is not time to waste. You
recognize that it is better to
take a step — any step — than
weigh forever what might happen
if the step is taken.

You do not hesitate in the
face of fear.

Aries, you step forward and offer
what you've got. You see the fear,
name the fear and proceed.
Fear has nothing on you. You
know how to take the first bold
step. That first tiny act is half
the battle.

You embody the spirit
of renewal.

You are always willing to start
over, dear Aries. When it gets
dark, you strike a match. When
you fall, you get up. You are
resilient. Yes, it can take a little
time to reach your goals. But the
spirit of renewal is alive in you.

♈

You plant seeds that grow
the garden of your life.

You are the Johnny Appleseed of
your life. You walk and you plant.
You sow seeds as you proceed and
trust wholeheartedly that the
right ones will bear fruit. Planting
the seeds is a delight unto itself.

You are forever creating the new.

Where there was nothing, now there is something. You love that magic, Aries. You love to birth the new. You love to conceive of the yet to be conceived. You pull new ideas from the top hat of your magical life.

You know how to fly solo when you need to.

You love to fly solo and you know how. Of course, you celebrate good company. But there's nothing like you and a project and the time you need. Certainly there will be collaboration, but Aries, you need time alone. Take it. Be fully in charge.

You love with fire,
with abandon.

You are hot and spicy. You
are passionate and bold. You love
to flirt. You love to pursue and
ignite. You love to reinvent
your relationships. You keep your
love alive.

♈

You are a forerunner.

You run ahead of the pack, explore the unexplored, go where no one has gone before, in thought or in action. You are entranced by the undiscovered and want to discover, see it and explore it first. You are a forerunner, Aries. Set off into your great beyond.

You know how to wing it.

Yes, dear Aries, you are spontaneous, enthusiastic and willing to improvise. Fire brings great creativity and unexpected journeys. If you are one who dives in, then winging it is required. But you relish the winging!

♈

You refuse the known route.

You are a bushwhacker, Aries.
The easiest route is not the one
for you. A new idea is exactly
that and you'll have to cover
uncharted terrain. The known
route is no fun. You want to
leave behind a path that
YOU created.

♈

You are a creative thinker.

Have we celebrated your smarts?
You have mental prowess. You
create and communicate the
new ideas we so desperately
need to heal our world. If we
could see beyond the physical,
there would be sparks all around
your head!

You are initiating fire.

Say that out loud! "I am initiating fire." Not much else needs to be said. You are a force of nature. You blaze. You begin.

Living Your Aries Love

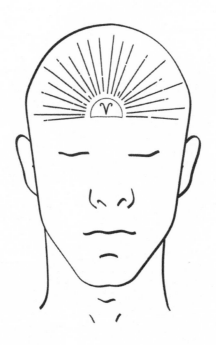

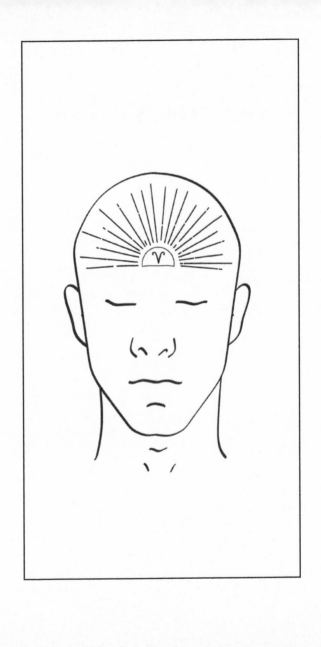

How are you feeling, dear Aries? Can you sense the potency of your gifts? Do you want to make the very most of this fiery energy of Aries? Here are some thoughts about how to live fully into your Aries Love and how to nourish your Aries Spirit. Consider them little whispered reminders meant to help you THRIVE. Consider them 'action items' — a loving Aries "to-do" list. Consider them invitations to live your fullest fire.

Wake up early and watch
the Sunrise.

Aries rules the dawn. The first
little glimmer of light will ignite
your fire. Feel the Sun rising in
you. Start your day watching the
light grow. Welcome the chance
to begin again. And then spend
the day carrying that light to
ignite all you meet.

♈

Spend time alone.

Go to lunch solo. Table for one please. Take a solo hike. Invite yourself for coffee and bring a good book. Recognize the beauty of your solo self — your strength and sovereignty. Feel yourself in the world unto yourself. Relish your solitude and all the bounty it brings.

Carve out time to think. Brainstorm.

That's right. Bring your computer or a journal to your favorite haunt and let loose. Write down all your inspirations or leave yourself memos on your phone. Make yourself available for 'lightning to strike.' New ideas need a recipient. Be ready.

Do something daily that requires your daring.

Make an important phone call.
Reach out and ask for support
with your next steps. Go beyond
your current physical comfort
zone. Summon your inner athlete.
Work out the muscles of daring.
Be willing to risk failure.

Strike the match
to light the fire.

Every tiny new idea is the spark
of something greater. Every
small step leads us closer to
the big dream. No step is too
small. No light is irrelevant. When
feeling blue, strike a real or
metaphorical match. Yes. Now
you've begun.

♈

Assert your Soul Self.

Stand for positivity in the face
of darkness. Step forth and
say what needs to be said. Let
everything good increase in you,
then offer it up. Go forth into the
world and offer your initiating
fire. You are here to blaze.

Apply your bravery to
a good cause.

Fight for the true, the good
and the beautiful. Use your fire
to inspire right action. Generate
ideas for the benefit of the
many. Be brave for those
who cannot.

Growing Your Aries Love

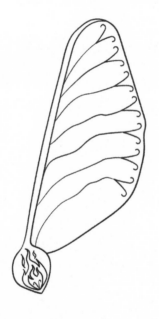

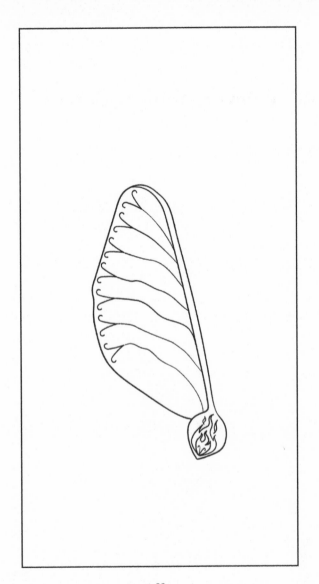

Sometimes, dear Aries, we swing too far in one direction and need to invite a balancing energy to set us right. We are all growing and need to address the parts of ourselves that have not developed as fully. The opportunity for Aries is to invite Libra (your opposite sign) into the picture. Here are ways to grow your Aries love to be more balanced, cooperative and peaceful.

Learn to Pause.

No one knows how to begin like you do, dear Aries. But occasionally, we need to take a moment to weigh the consequences of the leap. Your impulsivity can equally benefit or destroy. Occasionally, give yourself a moment longer to assess. You won't diminish your fire. You'll just add fuel to the right flame.

Don't give up on a great idea for the next new idea.

See your passions through, Aries. You have such a multitude of ideas but sometimes it's important to choose and give ONE your all. Don't allow yourself to get bored. Train for the marathon. Practice following through.

♈

Listen to the experience
of others.

Look outward. Listen outward.
Consider the opinion of others.
Listen to an alternative point of
view. Don't be so sure your way is
the only way. There are others
who have brilliant ideas. Give
yourself the time to listen.

Invite collaboration,
cooperation and consideration.

Sometimes you're lucky enough
to find the right partner, the
one who makes your idea
better. We often can act
alone and build something
gorgeous. But when we choose to
collaborate, something emerges
which we could never have
imagined. Invite others to play.

♈

Don't be a Bully.

I had to say it, dear Aries. It's easy to push too much. It's easy to fight too strongly for your own way. It's easy to overdo it as you forge forward. Assert wisely and with potent love.

♈

Cultivate patience.

Oh this one is hard. You move at quite a pace. It can feel like everyone else is moving in slow motion. Trust that there are a multitude of gifts in a slower pace. Trust that you are not behind or not missing out. You are right on time and there is no need to rush.

Practice long term commitment.

It's easy to abandon what feels old or known. You love the new after all. The grass is always going to look greener. But practice staying with what you love (and who you love!) to see if you can infuse the new. Don't be so quick to abandon what now feels stagnant. There are many ways to begin again.

Questions to Inspire
Sharing Your Aries Love

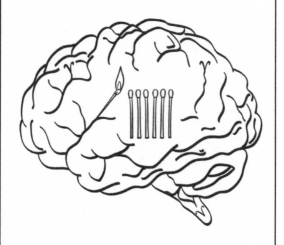

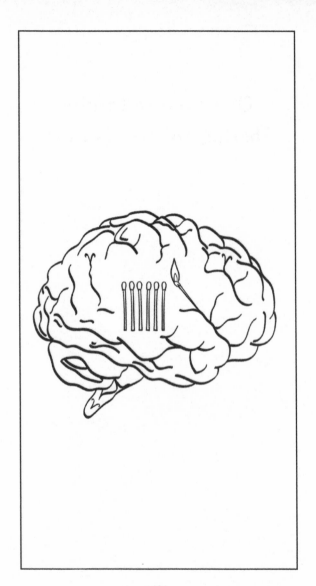

Dear Aries, here are a few questions and prompts that might inspire or clarify your mission. Grab your journal. Write for 15 minutes about each. Read your answers out loud to a friend. Let this exploration spark your next daring action.

What
is mine
to begin?

♈

Where
can I be
more bold?

♈

This is what I've been
thinking about lately,...

What is
one daring action
I can take today?

How
do
I
want
to
feel
NEW?

♈

What mission
do I want to assign
to my
warrior self?

What makes me feel
young and like everything
is possible?

Where am I fighting
that I don't need
to fight?

I feel impatient about...

I am willing to practice
patience here...

Who and what
needs my
initiating FIRE?

This is the first step
I will take...

One Last Little Love Note:

Aries, I hope these questions spark new possibility in your life. You have so much to offer, so much to give. And your fire inspires so many. If you ever need encouragement, just dip into this little book for a reminder of your light.

Now go forth Aries, and do your thing.

The World is Waiting for YOU.

Big love,
Heidi Rose

About the Author.

Heidi grew up with an astrologer father and an architect mother. Her father taught her the zodiac with her ABC's and her mother taught her to love art and appreciate the beauty of the natural world. She likes to call herself a poet with a map of the heavens in her pocket. Her passion is to inspire and encourage us all to be our truest, most authentic, radiant selves using the tools of astrology and poetry.

www.heidirose.com
Instagram @heidiroserobbins